# HEGGERTY HAGGER
# AND THE TREASURE HUNT

Story by Elizabeth Lindsay
Pictures by Peter Rush

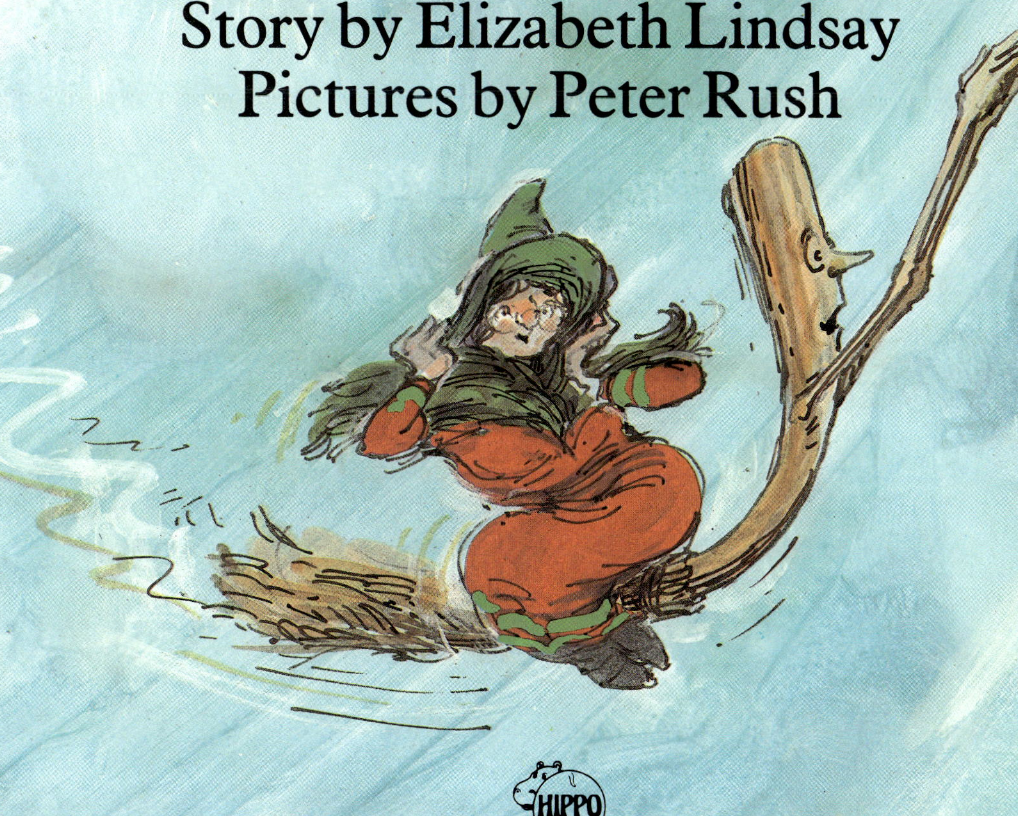

HIPPO

Hippo Books
Scholastic Book Services
London

For Emily

Scholastic Book Services,
10 Earlham Street, London WC2H 9LN, England

Scholastic Book Services Inc.,
730 Broadway, New York N.Y 10003, U.S.A.

Scholastic Tab Publications Ltd,
123 Newkirk Road, Richmond Hill, Ontario L4C 3G5, Canada

Ashton Scholastic Pty Ltd, PO Box 579,
Gosford, New South Wales, Australia

Ashton Scholastic Ltd,
165 Marua Road, Panmure, Auckland, New Zealand

First published by Scholastic Book Services 1984

Printed in Spain by Mateu Cromo, Madrid

Heggerty Haggerty lives in the cottage at the top of the hill. She has a broomstick called Broomstick and a black cat called Blackcat. As I expect you've already guessed, she's a witch.

Broomstick

One fine spring morning the sun streamed in through the sitting-room window as Broomstick sat down to breakfast. Blackcat lay on the hearthrug washing himself.

"What's this?" asked Broomstick, picking up a large envelope from beside his plate. His name was written in big letters on the front.

"It's for you. You'd better open it and see," said Heggerty Haggerty.

Broomstick held up the envelope to see if he could tell from the outside what was inside, but he couldn't so he opened it. "It's a big piece of paper," he said, shaking it onto the table. "What can it be?"

"Don't forget your egg. It'll get cold," said Heggerty Haggerty, smiling behind her teacup.

Broomstick spread the paper out on the table.

"There's a house, a farm, a lane, and a river. It's a map. I wonder who sent it?" he said.

"Blackcat found it on the doormat," said Heggerty Haggerty.

"There's some writing on the back," said Broomstick.

"It says 'Treasure Map'! A treasure map sent to me!" He could hardly believe his eyes.

"All treasure hunters need a good breakfast inside them," said Heggerty Haggerty wisely.

"Bother breakfast," said Broomstick.

Heggerty Haggerty picked up the map. "Breakfast comes first," she said firmly.

"Oh all right," said Broomstick and gobbled up his egg. He wanted to start treasure hunting straight away.

"I've got it," he said, pointing. "This is our house. This is Farmer Giles's farm. This is our lane, and this is our river." He turned the map over. "And this is the clue."

"Read it out then," said Heggerty Haggerty.

" 'Find your way to where the bucket squeaks down, then turn the handle round and round.' That doesn't make sense."

"It does if you think about it," said Heggerty Haggerty. "Where's there a place where the bucket goes down?"

"I don't know."

"Yes, you do. Think."

Broomstick screwed up his face and thought. "Got it!" he cried, and flew out of the door.

"Don't forget the map," called Heggerty Haggerty. "And wait for Blackcat."

Blackcat took the map in his mouth and scampered after him.

Broomstick whizzed down the garden and stopped in front of the old well. It wasn't used any more and usually had a lid on it. Today the lid was leaning against the wall. The wooden bucket that sat on the lid was gone and the rope was dangling down the well.

Broomstick and Blackcat looked over the edge. It was difficult to see down. The roof on the well kept the sunlight out.

"This is the place where the bucket squeaks down, and it is down," said Broomstick. "We've got to turn the handle round and round and pull it up again." He turned the squeaky handle and began to pull the bucket up.

"It's heavy," he said. "I bet the bucket's full of treasure." But the bucket, when it arrived, was full of water.

"It's full of water," said Broomstick. And he was just about to pour the water down the well when something at the bottom of the bucket caught his eye.

He put his hand in the water and pulled out a large, flat, shiny stone with writing on it. It was another clue. Broomstick read it out:

"Twirl to the left,
Twirl to the right,
Clap your hands three times
and see the rainbow's flight."

Blackcat looked at the map. He found the well marked by a small black cross. He couldn't see any other black crosses although he looked very hard.

"Come on, Blackcat," said Broomstick. "Fold up the map. We've both got to do this clue."

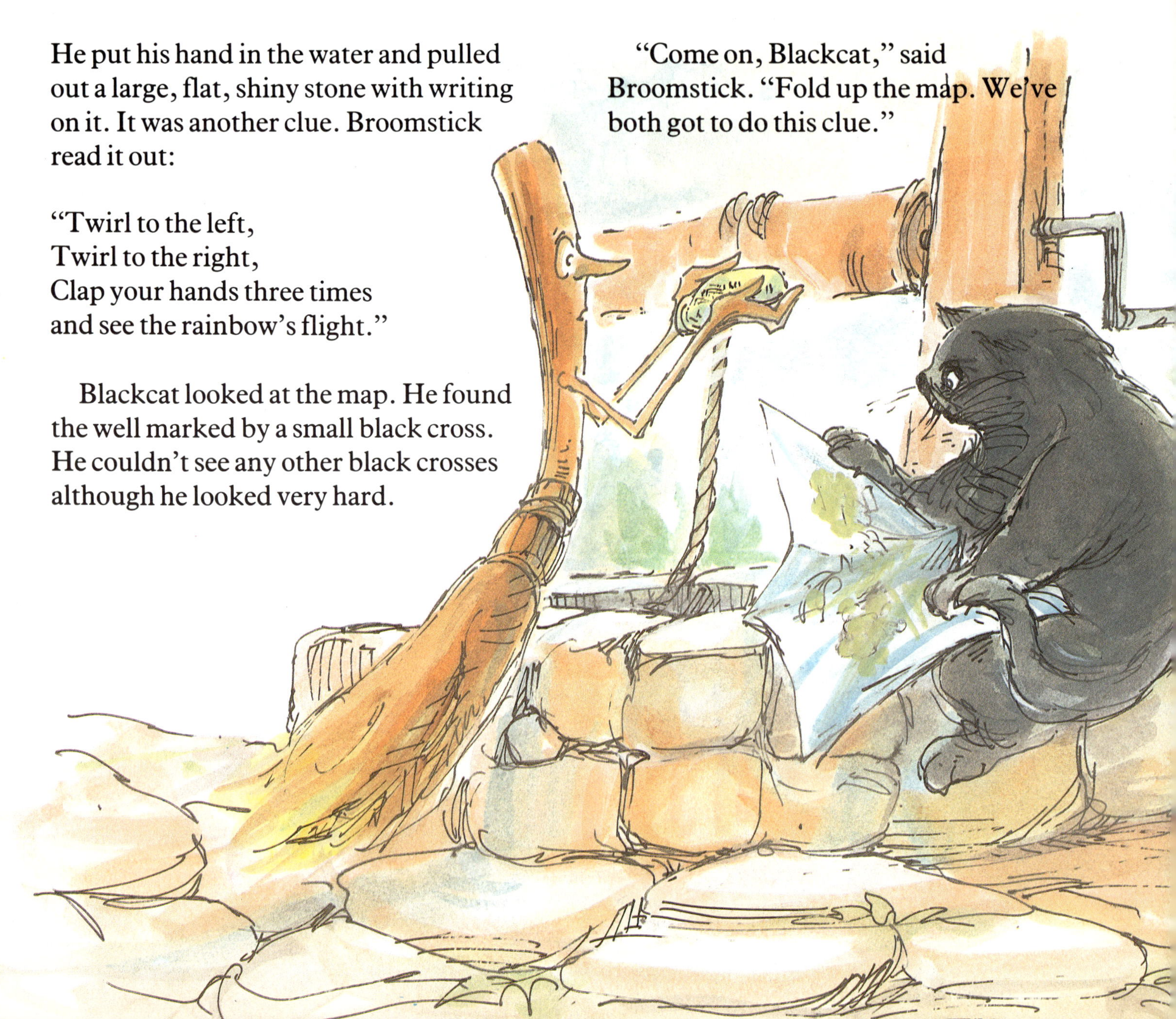

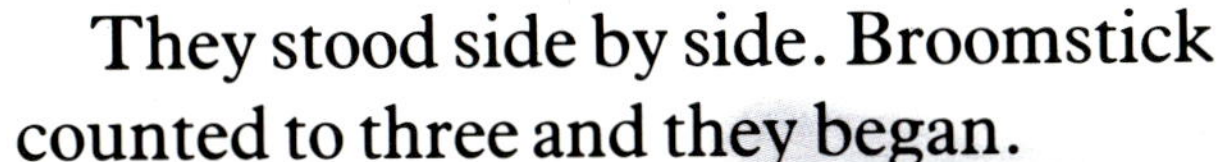

They stood side by side. Broomstick counted to three and they began.

"Twirl to the left,
Twirl to the right,
Clap your hands three times
and see the rainbow's flight."

When Broomstick said the last word, there was an orange flash and a rainbow-coloured streamer shot from the roof of the well. It flew down the hill towards Farmer Giles's farm. "Follow me" it seemed to be saying.

Broomstick, with Blackcat on his back, flew after the streamer as fast as he could go. They arrived in the farmyard just in time to see the rainbow streamer disappear into the barn.

"That's where the treasure must be," said Broomstick.

They both looked at the map and found the barn straight away. It was marked with a cross.

"Look," said Broomstick. "There's an arrow leading from the well down to the barn."

"That's jolly funny" thought Blackcat. "The cross was by the well before, and there wasn't any arrow either."

Blackcat followed Broomstick into the barn. It smelled sweet inside, made so by the piled-up bales of hay. They began searching, Blackcat on the ground while Broomstick flew above the hay and looked inside the big cart. They didn't find any treasure, or the rainbow streamer.

"I can't find anything anywhere," said Broomstick, giving up.

"Find what, old chap?" asked Farmer Giles, who was watching them from the doorway.

"Any treasure," said Broomstick. "We've got a map. We followed the rainbow streamer into the barn which was our clue, and now we've lost it."

"Well, I saw a rainbow streamer fly out through there," said Farmer Giles, pointing to the window at the end of the barn.

"So that's why we can't find it," said Broomstick. "Thanks, Farmer Giles."

They rushed outside.

When they got to the end of the barn they found the rainbow streamer pinned along the barn wall. Someone had painted the next clue on it in big black letters. Broomstick read it out:

"Mark fourteen paces to the apple tree,  
Then take six steps to where the beehive be.  
The flower pot marks the spot.  
Dig down deep until you are hot."

Broomstick called to Farmer Giles. "May I borrow your spade?"

"Help yourself," came the answer.

Broomstick grabbed a spade which was leaning against the barn and rushed over to Blackcat. "There's the apple tree," he said. "You pace, Blackcat. I'll count."

Fourteen paces took them nearly to the apple tree.

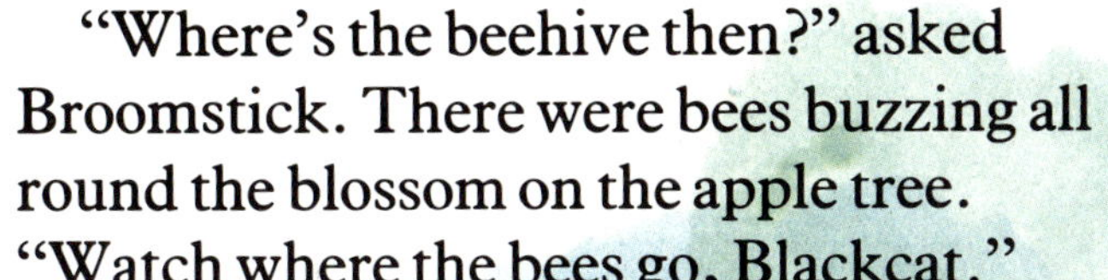

"Where's the beehive then?" asked Broomstick. There were bees buzzing all round the blossom on the apple tree. "Watch where the bees go, Blackcat."

The grass was tall and as they peered above it they saw the white top of the beehive on the other side of some brambles.

"Aren't we going to end up in the brambles if we take six steps to where the beehive be?" asked Broomstick. Blackcat shook his head.

Broomstick took six steps towards the beehive and ended up in a patch of earth with an upturned flower pot in the middle. "Blackcat, this is it!" he cried and he moved the flower pot and started to dig.

Blackcat looked at the map. The apple tree and the beehive were clearly marked and between the two was a large black cross. The arrow and the cross on the barn had disappeared!

Broomstick dug and dug, making a deep hole and a huge pile of earth. Blackcat kept checking the map to see if the cross had moved. It hadn't.

Suddenly there was a dull thud as Broomstick's spade hit something hard.

"I've found it!" he cried. "I've found it!" And he uncovered a small box which together they lifted out of the hole and slid on to the grass.

Broomstick was very excited. He struggled with the lock, opened it, and flung back the lid. "Treasure!" he cried. "Golden treasure!"

Broomstick picked up a handful of golden coins. But they didn't clink like proper money. Then he realised what they were.

"Chocolate money, Blackcat. Chocolate money treasure."

"How nice," sighed Blackcat, as he was rather fond of chocolate.

"Heggerty Haggerty must have made the map," declared Broomstick.

Blackcat thought so too. Magic rainbow streamers and vanishing arrows and crosses were just Heggerty Haggerty's sort of thing.

Farmer Giles lent them his wheelbarrow to carry the treasure home.

Heggerty Haggerty was waiting for them in the living room. "I see you've found the treasure," she said, smiling.

"The best treasure in the whole world," said Broomstick. "Chocolate money."

"Miaow," agreed Blackcat, heading straight for the hearthrug. "The best chocolate money treasure in the whole world." And he curled up for forty winks.